Hidden Treasures
of the
Egyptian Museum

Hidden Treasures
of the
Egyptian
Museum

One Hundred Masterpieces
from the Centennial Exhibition

Zahi Hawass

Photographs by
Kenneth Garrett
National Geographic Society

With a foreword by
H.E. Farouk Hosni
Minister of Culture

A Supreme Council of Antiquities Edition
The American University in Cairo Press
Cairo ⁓ New York

Copyright © 2002 by
The American University in Cairo Press
113 Sharia Kasr el Aini, Cairo, Egypt
420 Fifth Avenue, New York, NY 10018
www.aucpress.com

This publication was made possible through the support
of the National Geographic Society

Dar el Kutub No. 17364/02
ISBN 977 424 778 7

Designed by Andrea El-Akshar/AUC Press Design Center

The façade of the Egyptian
Museum, the predominant
architectural landmark on
Cairo's busy central Tahrir
Square, has beckoned millions
of visitors from around the
world for the last hundred
years; the neoclassical
structure was designed by
the renowned French

Contents

Foreword

H.E. Farouk Hosni

The Egyptian Museum constitutes an invaluable collection of ancient masterpieces that have resisted destruction: these priceless treasures have long surpassed their material being to reach a higher level of historic meaning to last as long as time. The uniqueness of the Egyptian Museum lies in its message to its cultured visitors, who will understand after their tour how the ancient Egyptian civilization propels us powerfully toward a better future.

The museum is a rich reserve of civilizational accomplishments in art, science, and literature, which the ancient nation-builders strove to achieve, leaving for history a secure legacy that will live forever. Thus this is not only a celebration of the first centenary of the Egyptian Museum but the shedding of a new light on the contents of the Museum, which continue to fascinate the world and are so alluring to scientists and researchers. And we will celebrate this great building once again when it becomes the unique holder of the rarest gems of Egypt's historic impression, on completion of the new Great Egyptian Museum near the Pyramids.

H.E. Farouk Hosni
Egyptian Minister of Culture

In the excitement of exploring the basement in preparation for the exhibit, Dr. Hawass and colleagues Dr. Ali Radwan and Dr. Mamdouh Eldamaty are enchanted with their first look at the cartouche of King Khufu inscribed inside this magnificent alabaster bowl found in 2002 at the Fourth Dynasty pyramid complex at Abu Rawash, north of Giza

A Celebration of
One Hundred Years
of the
Egyptian Museum

The Egyptian Museum is a portal through which the visitor is transported back to the mysterious realm of ancient Egypt: it holds the treasures of the greatest civilization in the world. It has been exactly one hundred years since the creation of the first permanent Egyptian museum. On December 9, 2002, at a centennial celebration, over 250 'hidden treasures' of ancient Egypt will be unveiled.

As the centennial of the Egyptian Museum approached I began to dream of an international celebration. I spoke with H.E. Farouk Hosni, the Minister of Culture, who encouraged the idea and added that the museum should have a face-lift for the occasion. The late Hamdi Shehata, head of Museum Sectors, Mamdouh Eldamaty, the director of the Egyptian Museum, and I began to plan renova-

tions for the century-old museum. The first item on our agenda: a new paint job for our somewhat faded exterior. Second: installation of an air-conditioning system to protect the collection from the ravages of temperature and humidity changes and enhance the experience of the visitor. Third: installation of exterior lighting to better exhibit our garden treasures to their full advantage. We put this plan into action, and then had another idea.

In the basement of the museum, unseen by the public, was a treasure trove of ancient artifacts. We thought that we should dig into them and choose the best one hundred artifacts for a new display. We thought that the mysterious basement rooms would also be a good place for the new exhibit.

When I looked at the artifacts from the basement, though, I was disappointed; they were not as magnificent as we had anticipated. I thought about the artifacts already on display in the museum: the diorite statue of Khafre, the builder of the second pyramid; the fabulous collection from the intact tomb of Khufu's mother Queen Hetep-Heres; golden treasures from the Middle Kingdom pyramids; the marvelous grave goods of the young king Tutankhamun; and the astonishing gold and silver funerary objects of Tanis. In fact, it seemed the previous curators had already selected the best artifacts, which were already on display in the halls of the museum, so we searched for another source for a new exhibit.

Suddenly I remembered that there were many artifacts, all over Egypt, that had been seen by no one but the excavators who found them, such as the beautiful statues discovered by Abdel-Moneim Abu Bakr in 1962 at Giza, which were neither published nor exhibited—in fact, they were still stored in a rock-cut tomb near the second pyramid! Between the best objects in the museum basement and the artifacts stored throughout the country, the number of objects on our list soon grew to 250. If we could somehow bring these treasures to the museum, we would be able to create an unparalleled exhibit to celebrate the Museum's one hundredth anniversary.

I asked Dr. Mohammed Abd el-Maksoud, head of the Pharaonic Section in the Delta and Dr. Mamdouh Eldamaty, director of the Egyptian Museum, for authority to open all the store rooms in Saqqara, the Delta, and Upper Egypt and to bring the artifacts that were languishing inside the magazines to Cairo. I obtained the cooperation of many foreign excavators to exhibit their stored artifacts for all the people to enjoy. I felt that this would help to bridge the gap between the first great scholars who contributed to the Museum—Mariette, Maspero, and Ahmed Pasha Kamal—and current excavators, both foreign and domestic.

Another committee was appointed to decide on the location of the exhibit. Among the members were Egyptologists and my friend the artist, Mahmoud Mabrouk. The Egyptologists felt that the exhibit should be inside the main hall at the Museum, but Mabrouk once again raised the idea of putting the exhibition in the basement. There was much objection to this idea, but I was intrigued by the idea of a unique and unexpected location, and the possibility of unveiling the Hidden Treasures of Egypt in an exotic setting. I called on Dr. Hussien el-Shabory, the architect who designed the museum at the new Bibliotheca Alexandrina, to see if he could design an exhibit that would be appropriate and overcome the objections. Dr. el-Shabory saw that an area running east and west, and located on the north side of the basement, could be quickly renovated and would be large enough to house the exhibit. So, after much deliberation by the committee, this location was agreed upon. The only problem now was time, and the task ahead seemed overwhelming.

The artifacts were collected from far and

wide, including areas in northern Egypt, such as Qiwesna, Tanta, Tell Basta, Gizira Mutawa, Kafr Hassan Dawud, Minshet Ezzat, Tell al-Dab'a, Mersa Matruh, and the underwater excavations in Alexandria. In Upper Egypt collection sites included Giza, Saqqara, Luxor, and Sohag. We put together a committee for the collection of the sought-after artifacts. The members traveled to the sites to transport the objects from the magazines—it was like *Mission Impossible*! The objects soon began to arrive in Cairo by car, truck, and airplane, and all within fifteen days of the beginning of the operation. I was constantly on my cell phone helping with logistical problems and reassuring worried committee members, not to mention the movers, the inspectors, and the foreign archaeologists who were concerned about the safety of their finds. However, arriving both day and night, the artifacts came to the Museum safely. The cooperation between all those involved was unprecedented.

Adventures in Transporting the Artifacts

One of the most exciting adventures was to bring the sarcophagus of Horwdja, dated to the Twenty-sixth Dynasty and discovered in 1992, from Qiwesna, fifty-seven kilometers north of Cairo. Horwdja, with his father and brothers, held the title of 'priests of the *Djed*-pillar at the House of the God [Osiris].' One of the most important scenes on the sarcophagus shows the family of the priest Hor-Djed. They

stand in front of the sacred tree with Isis and her sister Nephthys. Another beautiful scene is that of Anubis sitting in a mummification tent. On the sarcophagus are twenty-seven lines of hieroglyphs from the Book of the Dead, representing about eighty-nine chapters from the book. Made of black granite, and weighing approximately twenty tons, the sarcophagus is 241 cm long, 100 cm wide, and 145.5 cm high; moving it was going to be an enormous task.

The committee went to Qiwesna to see the sarcophagus. Tarek el-Awady, my assistant, took Ken Garrett, the *National Geographic* photographer, to make a photographic record of the adventure. Abd el-Hamied Kotb, chief engineer at the Giza pyramids, brought his team: Talal and Ahmed el-Kiriti, who are trained to move heavy objects. The el-Kiriti brothers have worked with me in moving heavy stones and sarcophagi on the Giza plateau. On first sight the committee thought the sarcophagus would be impossible to move because it was located on a seventeen-meter-high mound, and sat between mud-brick archaeological features. As the sarcophagus was located at the far end of the archaeological site, it was impossible to bring in any heavy equipment because the weight of the equipment would destroy the site. Everyone soon realized that the only way to move the sarcophagus was to transport it through a section of agricultural land adjacent to the site. Fortunately, the owner of the land agreed to let the workmen cross his land with the equipment. Using the same method as ancient Egyptian workmen, Abd el-Hamied Kotb's team tied the sarcophagus with ropes and pulled it onto wooden sledges. Using iron bars they dragged it while the workmen chanted, "*Salli aleeh . . . Salli aleeh*" ('pray for the Prophet'), to help with the rhythmic movement. First the lid, then the sarcophagus were loaded onto a truck for the ride to Cairo. The sarcophagus arrived at the museum, and the same method was employed to move it to its exhibit location, but on its arrival we discovered that it was too large to move into the exhibit space, so now it will be exhibited outside on the west side of the basement.

Another heavy statue came from the Delta, and will be exhibited next to the sarcophagus. It is a black granite statue of Horus in the hawk form, dated to the Late Period. The statue depicts Horus standing on a rectangular base designed for hieroglyphic inscription, although the artist chose to leave it blank. Superb detail, especially on the body of Horus, makes it one of the best sculptures of this period. Its height is about 122 cm and its width is 52 cm. The statue was in the garden of the Tanta Museum, but was never on display for the public.

The incoming artifacts were stored in another area of the vast basement, which became an interesting place for people to visit. Nadia Lokma and her team took on the restoration and conservation of the artifacts, and Ken Garrett spent many days photograph-

ing them for this catalog of the one hundred most interesting artifacts of the 250 objects selected for the exhibition, celebrating one hundred years of the Egyptian Museum.

Archaic Period Excavations
Early Dynastic Tombs in the Delta

The most important artifact in the exhibit from the Archaic Period is the Palette of the Solar Animals. It was discovered on land owned by a famous Egyptian composer, Kamal el-Tawiel. According to Egyptian law, artifacts or monuments on any land located near archaeological sites, or any land with evidence of antiquities or the possibility of discovery of antiquities is controlled by the government. If an individual purchases land and is aware of artifacts, or possible artifacts, then they may be responsible for the cost of excavation. The law states that the Director of the Supreme Council of Antiquities should appoint a committee to decide who will pay for the excavation. In this instance, although this property was owned by a prominent figure, the decision was made that this landowner must pay for the excavation.

Thus, in September 1998, in a village called Manshiat Ezzat, located near the town of Simbillaween in the Delta, the excavation, under the direction of archaeologist Salem Gabra el-Bagdady, began. A large cemetery was unearthed, with tombs dating to the First Dynasty, and to our great surprise the tombs

Talal and Ahmed el-Kiriti, known throughout Egypt
as the best team for handling heavy antiquities,
move the twenty-ton granite sarcophagus of Horwdja
using ancient Egyptian methods involving ropes,
wooden beams, and rollers; this Twenty-sixth Dynasty
masterpiece was found in a mud-brick cemetery at
Qiwesna in the Nile Delta

were rich with funerary objects. It is most likely the richest archaic cemetery recently discovered in Egypt. The beautiful palette was discovered in five pieces. When it was restored, it was found to be missing its top. The unique scenes on the palette depict animals such as a hunting dog and gazelles. In the middle of the palette are two animals facing each other, representing the unification of the two lands; their long curving necks form a circle representing the sun. The circle formed by the intertwined necks was used to mix kohl, an eye makeup used in ancient Egypt, so this palette probably sat on the dressing table of a wealthy Egyptian.

Old Kingdom Excavations

The Pyramid Builders' Cemetery in Giza

In 1990 excavations began at what was to revealed as the cemetery of the pyramid builders. The accidental fall of a horse's hoof through a hole uncovered the first tomb. The cemetery is located on a hill south of the pyramids of Giza. The first tomb excavated was a family tomb prepared with three false doors, the first for a man named Ptah-Shepsesu, the others for his wife and son. The tomb also contains a small open courtyard. The walls incorporate what appear to be left-over stones that were used in the construction of the pyramid, temples, and official tombs nearby. Nearly six hundred small tombs of a variety of styles and seventy more elaborate tombs were found at

this site. Up to two meters high, many tombs have pyramidal shapes, some are like beehives, and some have gabled roofs. Others have miniature ramps and causeways. In shafts under the tombs, simple rectangular burials contain skeletons of the owners, whose budgets did not cover mummification.

Many women are named in the inscriptions. It appears that the wives and daughters of the workers held positions as priestesses of Hathor or other goddesses. The statues and hieroglyphs indicate a family-centered lifestyle, wherein the construction of ceremonial centers and pyramids was looked upon as a labor of love and a national project. One statue of a beautiful seated woman named Hepeny-Kawes depicts her with large eyes and a well-modeled body under a long white robe. This is typical of Old Kingdom artistic representation. Found with Hepeny-Kawes was the figure of a woman grinding grain. She bends over her grinding stone, supporting her weight on well-muscled arms, while she rolls a heavy pestle over the grain.

During this excavation we discovered a ramp leading uphill to another cemetery. The upper level of burials is much more elaborate and contained artifacts and inscriptions, and the tombs themselves were constructed of stones of higher quality. Many of the skeletal remains were found in wooden coffins, although still not mummified. The tombs are much larger than in the lower cemetery. Some were made of limestone with mud-brick cores, others were rock-cut. Inscriptions in the tombs refer to overseers of the draftsmen, masonry workers, craftsmen, and one whose title was "The Director for the King's Work."

From this upper cemetery, and forming part of this exhibition, are the statues of Inty-Shedu. Cut into bedrock, and found intact, Inty-Shedu's tomb had a simple niche in the wall covered with mud brick. We noticed this because there was a small hole in the wall. I peered inside the niche with a flashlight and staring back at me were the eyes of a statue. A far greater surprise awaited me after I removed the mud brick covering the niche. Not one, but four statues now stared back at me. One large statue was flanked on the right by two smaller statues and on the left by another small one. We discovered the remains of a fifth wooden statue, which had stood at the far left. Disastrously, when we opened the tomb, the flow of oxygen caused it to disintegrate instantly. This wooden statue must have been added after the others were finished in order to accord with the ancient Egyptian appreciation of symmetry.

The four surviving statues are inscribed: "The overseer of the boat of the goddess Neith, the King's acquaintance, Inty-Shedu."

The faces of the statues were particularly interesting. After some debate we decided that the artist had depicted the boat builder at four stages of his life. The large statue in the middle is a portrait of Inty-Shedu just before his death. The two flanking statues characterize his youth, and the last on the right shows him at a younger age. The muscular features on each statue are representative of the age it depicts. The original five statues imitate the five statues of the pharaohs that were part of the pyramid temples from the time of Khafre to the end of the Old Kingdom. It was a thrilling discovery, and it was decided that H.E. Farouk Hosni should announce the discovery, but the 1992 earthquake interrupted the event, and the discovery has remained unannounced until now.

Other interesting tombs include that of Nefer-Theith and his primary wife, Nefer-Hetepes, his secondary wife, and eighteen children. The stela and three false doors are inscribed with beautiful hieroglyphs, and there are rare scenes of grain grinding and bread and beer making. Other scenes include depictions of fourteen types of bread, cakes, onions, beef, grain, figs, and a man making beer while another pours the beer into jars.

The tomb of a man named Petety is unique in its form. It has three open courts. The man and his wife, Nesy-Sokar, are depicted separately, probably because she was a priestess of the goddesses Hathor and Neith. Her tight dress leaves her breasts bare, and she wears a collar and a broad necklace. Her hair is divided in front of and behind her shoulders. Her head is tilted slightly up and forward, perhaps because of the wide, tight collar. The bold, confident expression is enhanced by the following threat: "Listen all of you! The priest of Hathor will beat twice any of you who enters this tomb or does harm to it. The gods will confront him because I am honored by his Lord. The gods will not allow anything to happen to me. Anyone who does anything bad to my tomb will be eaten by the crocodile, the hippopotamus, and the lion."

This pyramid builders' cemetery has been dated from 2551 to 2323 BCE, spanning from the Fourth Dynasty to the end of the Fifth. Eighty percent of the cemetery may still be under the sand along the hill. We believe today that many of the workers were conscripted farmers who would come to work during the time of the Nile inundation when working the farm was impossible. These workers are depicted in many paintings and reliefs. They are never depicted as slaves, and their style of dress and manner is that of peasants. The full-time workers are represented in the cemeteries, but part-time laborers were most likely buried in their various villages throughout Egypt, as they would have been returned to be buried with their families upon illness or accidental death.

Below the cemeteries, Dr. Mark Lehner is currently excavating a large section that from all appearances is the workmen's village. This may turn out to be similar to a New Kingdom site at Deir al-Medina, where areas for baking bread, salting fish, metal working, and craft shops were found, as well as paved roads and

dormitory-like rooms for sleeping: this is where the builders and artisans of the tombs in the Valley of the Kings lived from the sixteenth to the twelfth centuries BCE. It is thought that this type of organized labor was used on the pharaohs' monumental building projects. There is no evidence that slaves were ever used in the building of these monuments.

There is, however, evidence that the workers worked hard and suffered injuries. When comparing skeletons from the upper cemeteries and from the workers' graves, it is clear that the upper class were healthier and lived longer. Degenerative arthritis of the back and knees was more severe in the lower tombs. Simple and multiple fractures were present in both cemeteries, and most show signs of splinting, since they healed completely and with good alignment. Two cases of amputation healed correctly. Some skull fractures were noted. There is also evidence of emergency treatment of injuries by trained physicians, and one skull shows evidence of brain surgery. There is no evidence of mistreatment in the case of the workers.

The Tomb of the Dwarf, Per-ni-Ankhu

In the Western Cemetery at Giza there is a tomb that had been discovered by the American Egyptologist George Reisner. It had belonged to a man named Nswt-Nefret. Near this tomb is the tomb of the now famous dwarf Seneb, which had been discovered by the German Egyptologist Herman Junker in the

The Old Kingdom statue of a seated scribe sees the light of day for the first time in forty years; this statue is one of the finest pieces from a collection excavated in the Western Cemetery at Giza by famed Egyptian archaeologist Abdel-Moneim Abu Bakr, who passed away before he was able to publish his report of the discovery; the pieces have remained hidden in storage since 1962 in a rock-cut tomb near the second pyramid and are now being displayed for the first time in more than four thousand years last century. During the clearing of the accumulated sand around these tombs we discovered the Fourth Dynasty tomb of the dwarf Per-ni-Ankhu. This was exciting because it is one of only a few known tombs of dwarves. The tomb contained a statue of the dwarf of superb craftsmanship. Made of basalt, the sculpture is simple and clean. The dwarf is handsome, with a look of serenity, yet he exudes strength and power. He has a young face, yet he appears wise. On the right leg is an inscription: "He who pleases his majesty every day."

It is an unusual statue because basalt was usually reserved for royalty. This indicates that it was carved for Per-ni-ankhu by the royal sculptor, as opposed to a regular artisan. The statue reveals deformities in the subject's shoulders and legs, as is typical in dwarfism. When compared to the skeleton found in the burial shaft, the statue clearly demonstrates the type of sculptural realism common to this period. A study of the skeletons suggests that Per-ni-Ankhu was probably the father of Seneb.

The statue was accompanied by an illustration of the dwarf standing in the palace, and the phrase: "One known by the King, the dwarf in the great palace, Per-ni-ankhu." Climbing down into the tomb and holding the statue in my hand is a moment that I will never forget, although this discovery was followed by the excavation of sixty-five fabulous Old Kingdom tombs.

The Tomb of Kai

One of my favorite statues in the exhibit is that of the priest Kai, which was found inside his small, beautiful, and unique tomb. The tomb is so richly decorated that I call it the 'Nefertari of Giza.' At the entrance is an unusual inscription that reads: "It is the tomb makers, the draftsmen, the craftsmen, and the sculptors who built my tomb. I paid them beer and bread and made them to make an oath that they are satisfied."

Also at the entrance is a unique scene of Kai with one of his daughters. Her arms are placed affectionately around the neck of her father. This scene is the first of its kind from the Old Kingdom. Another scene shows Kai with his wife standing over several exotic-looking boats; the artist painted the background gray to cover his mistakes when drawing the boats and the people in them. Other scenes show daily life and an offering list with different kinds of wines and beers. The false door lists Kai's titles as the priest of Senefru, Khufu, Djedefre, and Khafre. Behind the false door is the burial shaft that contained a beautiful seated statue of Kai with his daughter and son flanking his sides. Inside the chamber were found the remains of two wooden sarcophagi and the skeletal remains of Kai. Interestingly, there was also a skeleton of a pig. We left Kai *in situ* out of respect for him and his beautiful tomb.

Beside this tomb we found another tomb built by Kai, this one for his daughters. The four walls bear beautiful scenes painted on plaster over mud brick. One of the scenes shows two daughters wearing banded dresses, and another shows a playful grayhound. On the floor is a circular limestone receptacle, which must have contained a decorated pillar. On it is a unique title: "One known by the king, the scribe, the *waab* priest and overseer of the places of the king's children: Kai."

The Pyramid of Queen Khuit and the Tomb of Tetiankh-Kem

At Saqqara, we discovered the pyramid of Queen Khuit near the pyramid of Queen Iput I. It is about seven meters high. Inside the pyramid was the sarcophagus and a room containing four canopic jars. Near it we found a funerary temple that consisted of a ritual room with three niches, a ritual chapel, and three other rooms. The wall reliefs of the temple give us an idea about the purpose of the wall reliefs in the funerary temples of the queens of this period. Scenes show the king with his mother, titles of the queen, and other scenes of the queen's activities in the afterlife, where she accompanies Hathor in a boat sailing in the marshes among lotus flowers. Offering bearers carry bread, beer, fruit, geese, vegetables, and meat that will be presented to the deceased and Hathor. There are also scenes of an early form of the *senet* game, and the song of *hfr*, which when sung enables the queen to defeat devils in the afterlife.

The discovery of the tomb of Prince Tetiankh-Kem near the pyramids of Iput I and Khuit provides important information about the beginning of the Sixth Dynasty Tetiankh-Kem, the eldest son of King Teti, died during the reign of his father at the age of twenty-five. Userkare became the king after the death of Teti, according to the lists of Abydos and Turin (he is not mentioned in the tombs of the high officials in the cemetery of Teti or in the Saqqara list). Userkare was not related to Teti, but apparently overthrew him. Later, the line was restored when Queen Iput I saw her son Pepi succeed to the throne. Pepi I changed the *mastaba* tomb of his mother to a pyramid to announce her status as Hathor Isis, which would help establish his legal right to the throne. This restoration of the royal line could also explain the disappearance of all the monuments of Userkare at Saqqara, and why he ruled for only a short period, an estimated seven years.

In the exhibit are two items discovered in the burial chamber of Tetiankh-Kem: the fabulous alabaster headrest and the tablet of the seven sacred oils. On the tablet is a line of hieroglyphics that reads: "The eldest son of the king, of his body, the sole friend, the honored one before the great God, Tetiankh." The seven sacred oils were used ritually both during mummification and afterward in funerary offerings. The seven oils—mentioned as early as the First Dynasty and as late as the First Intermediate Period—helped to seal the linen wrappings and were used in the Opening of the

Mouth ceremony, but unfortunately they helped quicken the deterioration of the bodies.

The plan of Tetiankh-Kem's tomb is simple, with an entrance on the southern side. The offering chapel has an inscription which reads: "The eldest son of the King, of his body, the hereditary prince, the count. The king's son, the seal bearer of the god, the chief lector priest. The scribe of the divine words, overseer of Upper Egypt, the sole friend. The overseer of the two granaries, keeper of Nekheb."

The chapel walls have scenes of offering bearers, butchers, and animals being slaughtered. A hall with the false door leads to a room at the entrance of which are depictions of servants in the act of dragging large vessels on wooden sledges. Other walls in this room show more offering bearers and a badly deteriorated depiction of the tomb owner with the scepter sign.

A shaft, which was filled with sand, has a simple entrance on the north wall of the hall. On the north side of the shaft is the burial chamber, which has three holes—possibly used by tomb robbers. An unpolished limestone sarcophagus lies directly under the false door located in the hall above. The lid of the sarcophagus was found raised up on stones, and a hole had been made in its edge and part of the base permitting perhaps a child to enter. Black soot remains where the thieves used torches to light their activity, and the mummy is in poor condition. Fortunately, the alabaster headrest and the tablet of the seven sacred oils escaped the attention of the thieves.

The Tomb of the Physician Qar

A happy accident brought about the discovery of the tomb of Qar, "the physician of the palace and keeper of the secrets of the king." Modern tomb robbers uncovered the adjoining tomb of Ny-Ankh-Nswt, which necessitated the immediate excavation of the area, and next to it was found the tomb of Qar. It consists of a small complex with a chapel and open court, a *mastaba*, burial shaft and chamber, and a wall surrounding the tomb. Although the sarcophagus had been opened, the skeletal remains tell us that the tomb owner was about fifty years old at death and was free of disease.

Several interesting artifacts were discovered in the tomb. Next to the head of Qar was a collection of copper surgical instruments, each with a hole used to hang it in a box; these are possibly the oldest surgical tools yet discovered. Other objects of bronze and wood, including a statue of the Third Dynasty architect Imhotep, were found in a cache outside the tomb.

A New Pyramid at Abu Rawash

While cleaning around the pyramid of Djedefre at Abu Rawash, a Swiss and Egyptian team discovered the substructure of a satellite pyramid. This small substructure held only two rooms, but surprisingly yielded a large, wonderfully made alabaster bowl. Inscribed on the inside of the bowl was the name of Khufu (Djedefre's father and builder of the Great Pyramid at Giza) in a cartouche.

The inscription is seen most easily with use of a light against the transparent stone.

In 1945, when Dr. Abdel Nomen Abu Bakr, professor of Egyptology, undertook an excavation of the western field of the pyramid of Khufu, he was forced to store many Old Kingdom statues in magazines and rock-cut tombs around the causeway of Khafre. I had been waiting for an opportunity to bring these statues out of storage since I saw them a few years ago, and I think Dr. Abu Bakr would be very proud to know that these statues have become a major part of the centennial exhibit. One of them is the statue of a scribe, which the Minister of Culture described as "dreaming." Other statues depict butchers, brewers, potters, and bakers. The statue of the baker is particularly interesting. It shows a man kneeling in front of his oven, his head turned to the left, and holding his hands in front of his face as if to shield it from the fire.

Middle Kingdom Artifacts

Representing the Middle Kingdom are statues and scenes with their own unique style. Many high officials' tombs are located in Beni Hassan and al-Bersha. One scene depicts thirty-seven bearded Asiatics in their native dress coming from the east.

In Middle Egypt, at al-Lisht, a new capital was established during the Twelfth Dynasty in order to extend the agricultural land. The kings of the Twelfth Dynasty, having learned from the past that pyramids had not protected their predeces-

sors' mummies, decided to build mazes of corridors out of masonry that would confuse would-be robbers. These corridors also represented the dark kingdom of Osiris. Traps were set along the corridors and the success of these was proven when early archaeologists unexpectedly happened upon the corpses of ancient tomb robbers hanging upside down by their legs. The cores of the pyramids built above the mazes are of mud brick, and they were covered with limestone from Tura. King Neb-Hepet-Re Mentuhotep, of the Eleventh Dynasty, built his tomb at Deir al-Bahari as a *mastaba* topped with a pyramid. From the mazes made here for the princesses Khnunet, Ita-Set-Hathor, and Meret come caches of jewels like lapis lazuli, amethyst, and carnelian.

A Twelfth Dynasty wooden cosmetic box in the exhibit comes from Qurna, and there are two Thirteenth Dynasty rectangular limestone stelae. One, in the name of a lady, Senet-It, was discovered at Abydos, which was the center for the worship of the god Osiris during the Middle Kingdom. Carved into the face of the second stela is a large ankh, which was a symbol of life—water, light, and air—all needed for the afterlife.

New Kingdom Excavations

The New Kingdom, dynasties Eighteen through Twenty, is considered the golden age of Egypt. Many of the six thousand artifacts from the tomb of King Tutankhamun in the Valley of the Kings have never been seen by the public, and some of these are included in the Hidden Treasures show. Recently restored gilded and inscribed leaves that decorated furniture, two painted wooden boxes, beautiful and extravagantly painted wooden boats, a golden pectoral, and a winged scarab holding the sun disk are among the newly restored artifacts. When the conservation team was working on a jewelry box from the collection, they were surprised to find inside it a piece of jewelry that had never been cataloged.

It was also in the Valley of the Kings that the amazing discovery of the famous cachette of royal mummies was made. When Heinrich Brugsch discovered the forty royal mummies, he removed them all to the museum, and some of them, like the famous mummy of Ramesses II, are now in the Mummy Room of the museum. What was never made public was the fact that there was a second cachette with thirteen mummies, three of which were left *in situ*. It is believed that they are the son of Amenhotep II, who was twenty years old at death; Mery-Re-Hatshepsut, main wife of King Thutmosis III; and Queen Ti, the wife of Amenhotep III and the mother of Akhenaten.

Between the cachettes of mummies was discovered a quartzite statue of Sebti, priest of the god Montu during the reign of Amenhotep III. Sebti kneels in a position of adoration and holds a small shrine that contains a miniature statue of Montu in the form of a falcon. This piece was recently retrieved from the Netherlands, where it had been lost for many years.

From the tomb of Aperia at Saqqara, which Alain Zivie discovered under the antiquities department resthouse, is a beautiful and unique ivory sculpture of a fish. The fish was a religious symbol representing the rebirth of the sun. Also from this tomb is a wonderful head, carved of wood, representing the wife of Aperia, who was the vizier of Egypt.

Also in the exhibit is a limestone sphinx of Ramesses II in full pharaonic regalia. Interestingly, this sphinx has human hands instead of paws, and is holding a jar. The sphinx was found among the many statues in the Karnak Cachette discovered in 1902. The history of this discovery is interesting. In 1899, eleven pillars collapsed in the hypostyle hall of Karnak Temple. Gaston Maspero appointed G. Legrain to restore the pillars in the temple. During reconstruction a hole was discovered in the northwest corner of a court that had been built by Thutmosis III. Covering the hole were stone blocks with inscriptions that dated to the Middle and New Kingdoms. By 1902, Legrain had uncovered over a thousand statues, and, astoundingly, he continued to discover statues, some 17,000 bronze, wood, and stone artifacts until 1905. The danger posed to the excavation by the rising water table caused the remaining artifacts to be left *in situ*, where they remain today. This cachette is still the largest find of statues ever made.

A prosthetic big toe dated to the Third Intermediate Period discovered still on its mummified foot was among artifacts recovered from the Luxor tomb TT 95, which was built during the reign of Amenhotep II. It was discovered in debris inside a shaft. The foot shows evidence that the amputation was cleaned and prepared for the device, and the site of amputation healed completely, which indicates that the owner lived long after the accident using the prosthesis.

Many Old Kingdom tombs hold treasures from the New Kingdom, the evidence suggesting that they were reused as chapels, tombs, and living quarters. During the cleaning of the Second Dynasty tomb of Nyneter at Saqqara in 1986, a group of statues was discovered, one of which is the double statue of the Memphite priest Amun-Emibt and his wife. Dated to the Nineteenth Dynasty, the statue is of fine limestone and artfully recreates the couple's fabulous clothing and headdresses of the couple. At Abydos, among the burials of the kings of the First and Second Dynasties, the upper part of a statue of King Seti I, the second king of the Nineteenth Dynasty, was discovered by W.M.F. Petrie at the Osirion behind the temple of Seti I.

In Umm al-Rakhem, twenty-eight kilometers west of Mersa Matruh, a statue of the military general Neb-re was discovered in 1994 by a Liverpool expedition in cooperation with Egyptian archaeologists. This statue dates from the time when Ramesses II was building military forts on the edge of the Delta in an effort to protect the borders from attack by the Libyans. Also found was a chapel that contained statues of Ptah, the god of the artisans, and Sekhmet, the goddess of war.

Underwater archaeology began in Alexandria in 1993 and this is the source of the wonderful statue of Isis found by Frank Goddio in cooperation with Ibrahim Darwish. The statue was found in four pieces and restored by Nadia Lokma and her team, along with several other gold artifacts. The statue may be the most beautiful statue of Isis yet recovered.

Excavations in the Bahariya Oasis

Bahariya is one of the five oases of Egypt's Western Desert. One day I received a call from Bahariya to tell me that I should visit the excavation there. When I looked into the first tomb and saw so many mummies, with gold covering their upper bodies, I was thrilled. This site became known as the Valley of the Golden Mummies, and the media coverage has been greater than at any other excavation in recent times.

There began to be a lot of pressure to allow tourists to see the site, and I started to worry about keeping the tombs safe from harm. I amended my usual position of not moving mummies from their resting places, and decided to move five to a nearby museum. Of these five, two are of children. That of the girl is in an exquisite sarcophagus; her gold mask is smiling. The boy's face is covered in a mask decorated with garlands in the style of the time. The merchants of Bahariya had become rich

Ahmed Orabi reassembles fragments of
the base of the late Eighteenth Dynasty
black granite anthropoid coffin of Senqed
from Saqqara in a temporary workshop
set up for the purpose in the dark corridors
of the Museum basement

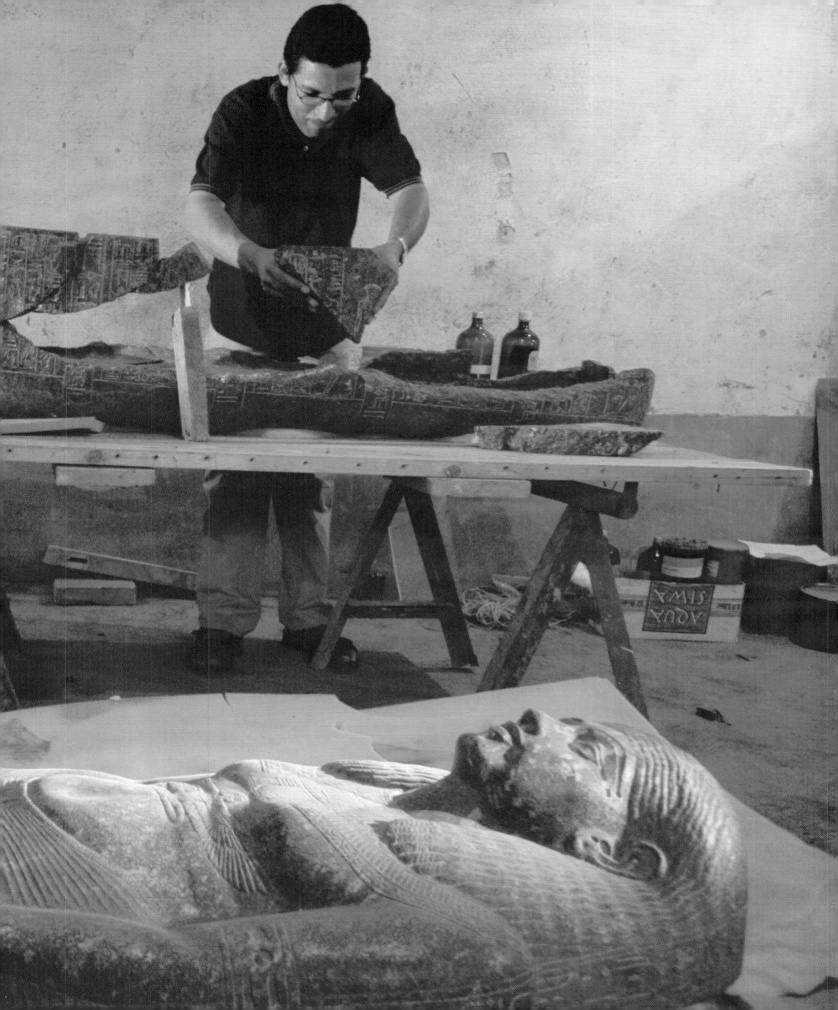

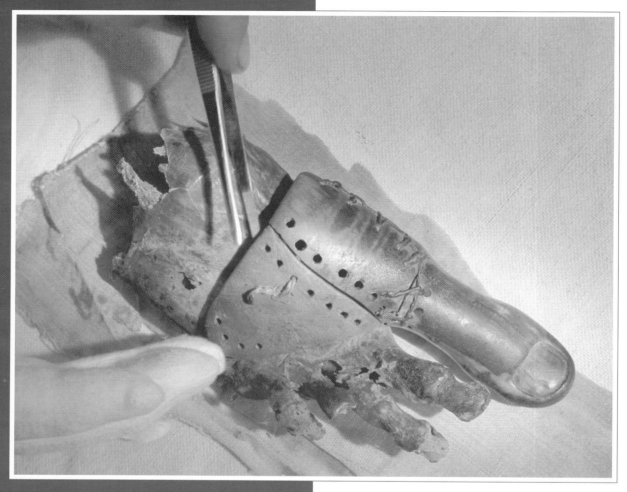

Conservators work on the wooden artificial toe with leather attachment found on a mummified foot dated to the Third Intermediate Period and retrieved from the debris in a New Kingdom shaft at Qurna, Luxor, in preparation for the exhibit; careful examination of the toe and the foot shows that the prosthesis was worn by the owner in life

through their trade in wine with Upper and Lower Egypt, and so were able to cover their mummies with gold.

The other exciting find at Bahariya was a temple built for the god Bes, and a splendid statue was recovered from this site. The domestic deity Bes was a popular figure who had an ugly face with the ears and mane of a lion and a headdress of tall plumes. He bares his teeth in an ugly grimace, and can be frightening, but he is also rather comical. He was the god of joy, sexuality, dancing, and music. Since Bahariya was a center for wine production, the people's adoration of Bes is understandable.

In Bawiti, the capital of Bahariya, a surprise waited under one of the modern houses. Two young Egyptians came to see me at the excavation of the golden mummies and they told me that they knew that there was a tomb under a certain house. They led me into the house, and through to the bathroom. In the bathroom floor was a hole. I climbed down into the hole, which was ten meters deep, and I couldn't believe my eyes. This was the tomb of a governor of Bahariya in the Twenty-sixth Dynasty, Djed Khonsu Iuf Ankh.

The tomb contained a large sarcophagus, weighing sixteen tons. All around it was a foul-smelling yellow powder, a half-meter deep. It took my team two weeks to remove the powder, which turned out to be ground hematite, which was often used as a pigment, but why the people chose to pour it around the tombs is still not understood. After clearing out the powder we decided to lift the lid of the sarcophagus, which was so heavy it took five hours to move. We found another sarcophagus of alabaster inside the first, and inside that was a third made of limestone. When we moved the limestone sarcophagus, we found under it the remains of a wooden sarcophagus. Here there was a deteriorated mummy with nine gold amulets, which are included in the exhibit.

North of the governor's tomb was the tomb of his wife, Nasesa II, whose sarcophagus contained 103 pieces of gold. The third tomb in the maze belonged to the governor's father Badi. Before this excavation was over we had to demolish twenty houses and relocate the residents—it took us three months to clear the site.

The Supreme Council of Antiquities would like to express its appreciation for the contribution made through the ages by foreign scholars like Auguste Mariette, Gaston Maspero, Heinrich Brugsch, Amelia Edwards, Flinders Petrie, and a host of others; they filled the museum with magical, awe-inspiring artifacts that have captured the hearts of people all over the world. We also recognize scholars like Rifaa al-Tahtawi, Ali Mubarak, and especially Ahmed Pasha Kamal, whose passionate love of their country broke down political barriers that had prevented Egyptians from fully appreciating their own history. We recognize political leaders like Mohammed Ali, Khedive Said, Khedive Ismail, and Khedive Tawfiq, whose efforts to modernize Egyptian archaeology helped to stem the loss of artifacts, and create conservation and educational programs.

We acknowledge the efforts of archaeologists, scholars, and politicians from around the world who believed that Egypt should control its own destiny. We are grateful to all those involved in the wonderful new renovations, and the new exhibition, and together we proudly celebrate the one hundredth birthday of the Egyptian Museum.

History of the Museum

1835 Mohammed Ali, in an effort to stop the plundering of antiquities by foreign collectors and to cultivate more interest in Egypt, asks Yusuf Diya Effendi to propose a site for an Egyptian museum in Azbakiya, and asks the Minister of Education to make a full report, documenting the archaeological sites, and to assure that the artifacts are sent to the store rooms in Azbakiya. The death of Ali stalls the progress.

1848 In order to protect the artifacts, Khedive Abbas I moves them to a hall in the Citadel. Austrian Duke Maximillian visits the collection and is so impressed that Khedive Said gives him the collection as a gesture of good will.

1855 Khedive Said orders the police to be more vigilant in watching for Egyptian antiquities being sold or exported. Auguste Mariette hurriedly excavates at Saqqara and discovers the Serapeum. Most of the artifacts discovered there are taken away secretly to France.

1858 Khedive Said establishes the Egyptian Antiquities Service and appoints Auguste Mariette as the first head. Mariette begins a program to document excavations, and attempts to take up the failed project of Ali to establish a formal museum. Due to lack of French and Egyptian funds, he renovates an old mosque in Bulaq to be used as a temporary museum, collecting pieces from various storerooms around Egypt.

1859 Draa Abu al-Naga: The intact tomb and treasures of Queen Iah-Hotep are discovered by Mariette; her sarcophagus captures the heart of Khedive Said.

1863 Khedive Said finally orders that an Egyptian museum be built in Bulaq. It opens during the reign of Khedive Ismail.

1869 Ali Mubarak and Heinrich Brugsch establish the first school of Egyptology in a villa near the Bulaq Museum. It closes in 1874 due to Brugsch's absence and Mariette's hostility, which derails Egypt's first attempt at training its own Egyptologists.

1878 The Bulaq Museum, built on the Nile, is flooded and severely damaged. Mariette begins to ask authorities for a better and more permanent location for a museum.

1879 Rifaa al-Tahtawi returns from his studies in Paris with a new philosophy: improve the national consciousness of Egyptians and awaken their appreciation of their ancient monuments. He succeeds in inspiring several young scholars who believe that Egyptians should be included in their country's archaeological work.

1881 The month that Mariette passes away, he extracts a cabinet resolution that "Hereafter no Egyptian monument shall be given to any power . . . not forming a part of the Egyptian territory." Gaston Maspero succeeds Mariette as head of the Egyptian Antiquities Service. Ahmad Kamal graduates in France and carries on the work of increasing awareness about the Egyptian heritage. Maspero shows his respect for Kamal by including him in the group that publishes the *Catalogue Général*. Kamal opens a tiny school of Egyptology at the Bulaq Museum. The government provides funds for five students, but when they graduate, it uses the money to pay their salaries as antiquities inspectors instead of funding further students. Due to lack of funds the school closes in 1885.

1887 The Bulaq Museum is very crowded; many artifacts are stacked against walls or being stored in boats in Upper Egypt after they are excavated. Sarcophagi are stacked one upon the other. The situation is desperate, and finally the Khedive donates one of his palaces at Giza for a new museum.

1890 The new museum at Giza is opened, but it is still not large enough. Eventually Khedive Tawfiq decides to build a new museum in Cairo. He announces an international competition for the best architectural plans. Seventy-three projects are submitted. The winner is French architect, Marcel Dourgnon. The Italians are awarded the contract for the museum's construction, perhaps as consolation for losing the competition.

1897 Construction of the museum begins. This is the first purpose-built museum in the world. Among those present at a festival for the new museum are the reigning Prince Abbas Hilmi and Gaston Maspero, who has returned as Director of the Antiquities Department.

1901 The key to the museum is given to Italian architect Alessandro Barasanti and he begins, in March 1902, to move the objects from the palace in Giza, the old museum in Bulaq, and the Azbakiya storage houses. Five thousand wooden carts are used to haul the treasures. The first load contains about forty-eight stone sarcophagi weighing about one thousand tons. It is difficult and dangerous work. The officials notice that the statue of Kin Hor is missing and a vigorous search begins. When it is discovered in a corner of the new museum, behind other objects, frightened workmen admit that they had accidentally damaged the statue and then hidden it in an effort to avoid punishment.

1902 The new building is completed and the artifacts are in place. Even though the design is neoclassical, and the exterior reflects not one Egyptian contribution, *inside* the pharaonic influence persists. The halls are similar to the pylons at the ancient temples, and the rooms are amazingly like the rooms in the temple at Edfu. In the basement rooms, Ahmad Pasha Kamal, the first Egyptian Egyptologist, works with quiet dignity to break down the barriers that keep Egyptians out of archaeology. He and Ahmad Lufti al-Sayyid strive to prepare

Egyptians to manage their own archaeology. On July 13 the tomb of Mariette is moved to the new museum garden. His will had indicated that he wanted his body to lie near the ancient artifacts that he had struggled all his life to collect, protect, and properly exhibit. Maspero becomes the initial curator.

1910 Ahmad Kamal persuades the Ministry of Education to form an Egyptology section in the Higher Teachers College of Cairo. At the Egyptian University he teaches his third class on ancient Egypt. In years prior he published articles and books in Arabic and French about Egyptian archaeology, Arabic grammar, and history.

1922 The contents of the tomb of a young king named Tutankhamun are uncovered in the Valley of the Kings and for the first time Egypt retains all the artifacts of a site. Egypt takes control of all exportation, museums, antiquities, schools, and the training of new Egyptian Egyptologists.

1951 Ahmad Kamal is recognized as the first Egyptian archaeologist. His great achievements in Egyptology are honored by the placement of a bust made in his likeness in the garden of the Egyptian Museum.

2002 Centennial celebration of the Egyptian Museum. Museum renovations, complete with a new exhibition gallery in the basement, new exterior lighting, and a huge new parking facility are unveiled. The Supreme Council of Antiquities brings artifacts from all over Egypt to be viewed by the public for the first time. At last the hopes and dreams of generations of Egyptian and foreign scholars are being realized. The Museum's school of Egyptology, which struggled and failed so many times in the past, is scheduled to open in January, 2003. The children of Cairo are not left out: a school that will teach young Egyptians about their heritage, and the value of their antiquities, is opened at the museum.

Part of a palette
Slate
L. 10.5 cm; H. 10.5 cm.
Late Predynastic Period

The Predynastic and Archaic Periods

(Stone Age through Second Dynasty)
c. 5300–2686 BC

Stone tools found in the Western Desert testify to human activity in Egypt during the early Palaeolithic period around 300,000 years ago, when hunter–gatherers found plentiful plant foods and game in the savanna land that existed where there is now desert. The Predynastic Period began with climate change around 7,800 to 6,500 years ago, which saw aridity spread across the traditional hunting grounds, forcing these Neolithic people to move closer to the Nile. From about 5300 BC they began to settle in first Lower and then Upper Egypt, archaeological evidence revealing distinct cultural differences between north and south. Type sites identify these cultures as Qarunian (Fayum B), Merimdian (from Merimda Beni Salama), Omari, and Ma'adi in Lower Egypt; and Badarian, fol-lowed by the Naqada cultures (Amratian and Gerzean) in Upper Egypt.

The Badarian culture showed a variation in sizes of graves, quantity and quality of grave goods, which implies greater social stratifica-tion. Around 4000 BC the Badarian culture developed into the Naqada culture, the third phase of which is now identified as Dynasty 0, when there was a concerted movement from south to north to unite the country. Political power centered on several large settlements or towns, such as Hierakonpolis, Naqada, Abydos, and This. Religious as well as political concepts began to evolve that continued throughout the historical era, such as the identification of the king with the falcon god of the sky, Horus.

By about 3100 BC Lower Egypt had been completely taken over by the Upper Egyptian culture. Ancient tradition named Menes as the

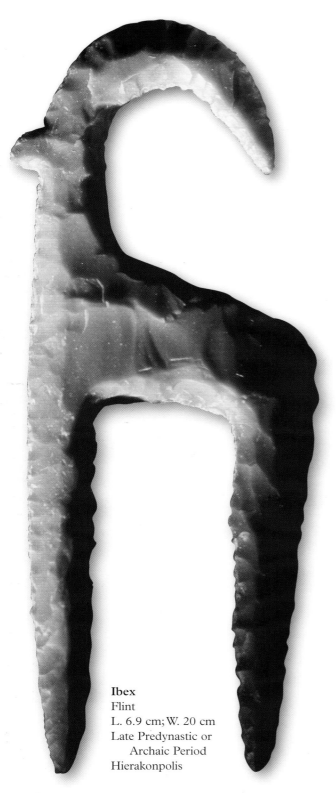

Ibex
Flint
L. 6.9 cm; W. 20 cm
Late Predynastic or
    Archaic Period
Hierakonpolis

king who first united Egypt and established the first of the thirty-one dynasties into which the history of Egypt was subsequently divided. He is probably to be identified with Narmer, last king of Dynasty 0 (whose famous ceremonial slate palette in the Egyptian Museum records the unification), or Aha, first king of the First Dynasty, who founded Memphis as the capital, at the meeting-point between Upper and Lower Egypt.

The formation of the Egyptian state begun in Dynasty 0 was consolidated during the Archaic Period (First and Second Dynasties). Principals of centralized government were laid down, cultural unity was achieved in social and religious customs, characteristics of art and architecture were formulated, and most important of all, the simple system of hieroglyphic writing was fully developed. There were increased trade links with Syria–Palestine to the northeast and Nubia to the south. The Horus-kings of the period were buried in magnificent mud-brick mastaba tombs at Abydos, and the ideology of the god–king unified the country for almost 800 years until the end of the Old Kingdom.

The tombs of princely high officials at Saqqara, the necropolis of Memphis, were comparable with those of the kings at Abydos. Grave goods included hundreds of pottery and stone vessels, the latter being a particular feature of this period, and displaying the consummate skill of the ancient artisan in the working of hard stone of all kinds, an art that was to continue throughout pharaonic history.

Mask
Pottery
L. 25 cm; W. 20 cm
Late Predynastic or Archaic Period
Hierakonpolis

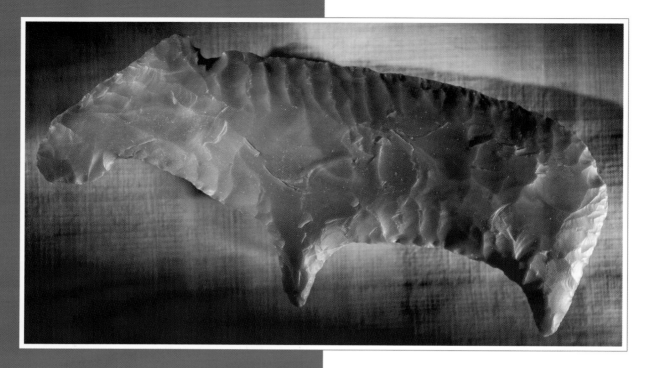

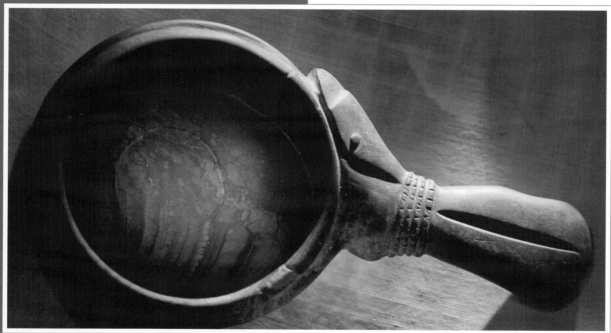

Schist spoon
L. 16.5 cm
Naqada 3 Period
Manshiat Ezzat, al-Simbillaween
Supreme Council of Antiquities excavation

△△ **Hippopotamus**
Flint
L. 11.3 cm; W. 4.9 cm
Late Predynastic or Archaic Period
Hierakonpolis

Palette of the solar animals
Schist
H. 23 cm; W. 21.5 cm; D. 0.8 cm
Dynasty 0 / Naqada 3 Period
Manshiat Ezzat, al-Simbillaween
Supreme Council of Antiquities excavation

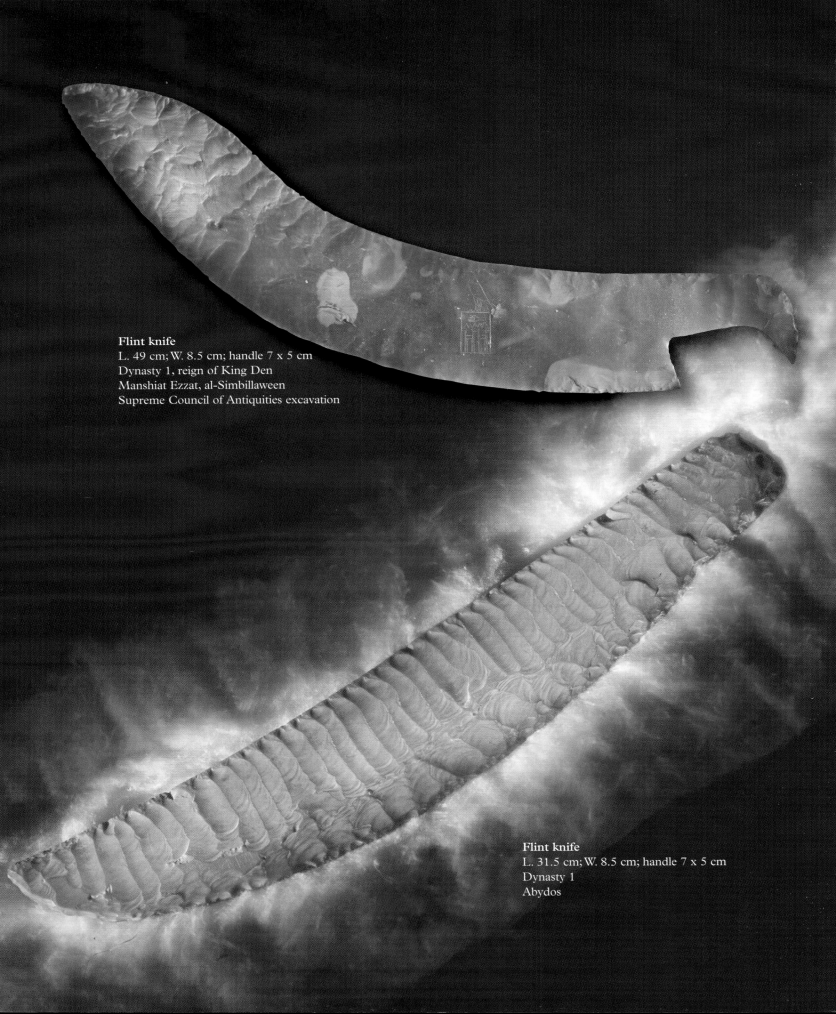

Flint knife
L. 49 cm; W. 8.5 cm; handle 7 x 5 cm
Dynasty 1, reign of King Den
Manshiat Ezzat, al-Simbillaween
Supreme Council of Antiquities excavation

Flint knife
L. 31.5 cm; W. 8.5 cm; handle 7 x 5 cm
Dynasty 1
Abydos

Four Labels
Bone
L. 4 cm
L. 3.6 cm; W. 3.3 cm
L. 3.6 cm; W. 3 cm
L. 3.8 cm; W. 3.4 cm
Dynasty 1, reign of King Qaa
Abydos

Wavy-handled jar
Alabaster
H. 30.6 cm; diameter 13 cm
Dynasty 3
Djoser Pyramid, Saqqara
CG 88276

The Old Kingdom
and the
First Intermediate Period

(Third to Eleventh Dynasties)
c. 2686–2040 BC

Often called the 'Pyramid Age,' the Old Kingdom of the Third to Sixth Dynasties witnessed the building of the first monumental stone structures, the royal pyramid complexes, and private mastaba tombs, many of which were never surpassed in size and grandeur. The first pyramid, the Step Pyramid of Djoser (second king of the Third Dynasty) at Saqqara, was surrounded by a huge complex of temples, shrines, and courts. Although Sneferu, first king of the Fourth Dynasty, constructed three pyramids, his Northern Pyramid at Dahshur being the first 'true' pyramid, the apogee of pyramid building was reached in the reign of his son and successor, Khufu, owner of the Great Pyramid at Giza, one of the Seven Wonders of the Ancient World.

The royal title 'son of Re,' the sun-god, was adopted in the Fourth Dynasty, reflecting the increasing dominance of the cult of the sun. The royal cult was assimilated with that of Re in the Fifth Dynasty, when the kings built individual sun-temples near their pyramids. Although textual material is scarce from the early Old Kingdom, more survives from the later dynasties of the period. The Pyramid Texts and the Abusir Papyri provide evidence of religious beliefs regarding the royal hereafter, and the administration of the mortuary temples. Tomb autobiographies provide information on the political, social, and economic circumstances, such as military campaigns and trading expeditions to Nubia and Western Asia.

Reasons for the breakdown of the Old Kingdom at the end of the Sixth Dynasty are still a matter of debate. Possibilities include climate change with lower annual rainfall and series of low Nile floods, which brought economic chaos, famine, and political unrest. The increasing power and independence of the provincial nobility and a decrease in royal wealth through tax exemptions for funerary endowments have also been suggested.

The First Intermediate Period, which covers the Seventh to Tenth Dynasties, was the first of three periods in Egyptian history when the centralized government broke down and the unity of the kingdom was disrupted. The Seventh and Eighth Dynasties continued to rule from Memphis, but the kings had very short reigns, eighteen to twenty kings ruling over a period of thirty years. The Ninth and Tenth Dynasties ruled from Herakleopolis, near modern Beni

Suef, but their authority was confined mainly to the northern region, as they were opposed by the Theban rulers of the early Eleventh Dynasty.

The lack of major building works and royal funerary monuments from this period makes it difficult to assess the political situation. The exploits of provincial governors and their allegiance to the Herakleopolitans or the Thebans are described in their tomb inscriptions at such sites as Asyut, al-Mo'alla, and Gebelein. They enjoyed a certain degree of autonomy, and even kept private armies. The Theban king Mentuhotep II eventually succeeded in reuniting the country, although whether by military force or by diplomacy, or by a combination of these policies, is not clear.

**Offering-table of a woman
called Ankh-Nes**
Limestone
L. 37cm; W. 25cm
Old Kingdom
Egyptian Museum CG 154521

The dwarf Per-ni-ankhu seated
Painted basalt
H. 48 cm; W. 14 cm
Dynasty 4
Tomb of Per-ni-ankhu, Giza
Hawass excavation, 1990

11

Four statues of the artisan Inty-shedu
Painted limestone
Seated: W. 26 cm; H. 75 cm; base 27 cm
Seated: H. 40.5 cm; W. 12.2 cm
Seated: H. 32 cm
Standing: H. 31 cm; W. 5.8 cm
End of Dynasty 4
Tomb of Inty-shedu, Giza, workmen's cemetery
Hawass excavation, 1992

Statue of Kai
Painted limestone
H. 56 cm; W. of base, 25 cm
End of Dynasty 4
Tomb of Kai, Giza
Hawass excavations, 1992

Statue of a woman called Nefret
Painted limestone
H. 43 cm; W. of torso 12 cm
Old Kingdom

Statues discovered at Giza in the
Cairo University excavations
Dynasty 5

Double statue of a man and his wife
Painted limestone
H. of man 65 cm; H. of wife 51.5 cm
Dynasty 5
Giza
Cairo University excavation

Statue of seated scribe
Painted limestone
H. 46.5 cm; W. of torso 23.5 cm
Dynasty 5
Giza
Cairo University excavation

Kneeling statue of a priest offering Nu-Jars
Limestone
H. 33 cm; W. 15 cm
Dynasty 5
Giza
Cairo University excavation

**Headrest of Teti Ankh Kem; offering tablet
of the seven sacred oils**
Alabaster
Headrest: disc diameter, 8 cm; H. of pillar 12.6
    cm; diameter of pillar top, 5.7 cm; diameter
    of pillar base 7.6 cm
Tablet: L. 16.5 cm; W. 7.7 cm; D. 1.5 cm
Beginning of Dynasty 6
Saqqara, King Teti Cemetery
Hawass excavation

Offering table of Qar
Alabaster
Diameter 31.5 cm;
     H. of base 7 cm
Dynasty 6
Saqqara
Hawass excavation, 2001

Stela recently returned from New York
Limestone
H. 59 cm; W. 95 cm
Old Kingdom

20

The double statue of
Pen-Hesy Meru
Painted limestone
H. 56cm
Old Kingdom
Nag al-Mashaykh
Egyptian Museum CG 15600

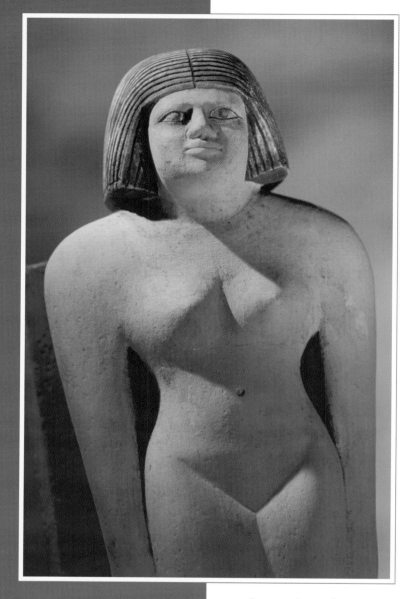

Statue of standing woman
Painted limestone
H. 47cm; W. of torso 15cm
Old Kingdom
Giza
Cairo University excavation

▷ **Statue of standing man**
Painted limestone
H. 59cm
Old Kingdom
Giza
Cairo University excavation

Alabaster bowl with cartouche of King Khufu
Diameter 52 cm
Old Kingdom
Abu Rawash

Canopic Jar
Alabaster
H. 25 cm; W. 20 cm
Old Kingdom
Abu Rawash

Two statues
Wood
H. 17 cm
H. 13.4 cm
Old Kingdom
Abusir

Seated statue of Nefer
Limestone
Old Kingdom
Abusir

False door with the cartouche of King Unas
Limestone
H. 69 cm; W. 46 cm
Old Kingdom
Saqqara
German excavation

Canopic jars in the form of the Four Sons of Horus
Alabaster
H. baboon: 43 cm; jackal: 45 cm; human: 50 cm; falcon: 53 cm
Old Kingdom
Tell Basta

**Double standing statue of a man
    and his wife**
Painted limestone
Man: H. 65 cm; W. 16 cm
Wife: H. 63 cm; W. 8 cm
Old Kingdom
Giza
Cairo University excavation

Funerary stela of Shedetef
Painted limestone
H. 60 cm
First Intermediate Period
Nag al-Mashaykh
SR 15765 / TR 19/1/24/2

Cosmetic box
Wood
L. 9 cm; W. 7 cm; H. 6 cm
Early Middle Kingdom
Qurna
SR 1769/JE 3318

The Middle Kingdom
and the
Second Intermediate Period

(Eleventh to Seventeenth Dynasties)
c. 2040–1550 BC

Defined as the classical period of ancient Egyptian history, the Middle Kingdom saw great achievements in art, architecture, craftsmanship and literature. Amenemhat I, first king of the Twelfth Dynasty, was the vizier of Mentuhotep IV, last king of the Eleventh Dynasty. He founded a new capital near modern al-Lisht, named *(Amenemhat) itj-tawy*, '(Amenemhat) seizer of the two lands,' the exact location of which is still unknown.

During the early Twelfth Dynasty the administration was consolidated with the clarification of the boundaries of the nomes (provinces). Agricultural land was expanded in the Fayoum oasis, a favorite region for the Twelfth Dynasty kings.

Lower Nubia was taken over to provide a buffer zone between Egypt and the prominent Nubian kingdom of Kerma between the Second and Third Cataracts. A channel was dug through the First Cataract at Aswan to ease river traffic, and to maintain control over Nubia massive mud-brick fortresses, masterpieces of military architecture, were constructed at strategic points. Texts refer to a similar defensive line, the 'Walls of the Prince,' along Egypt's northeastern frontier. Commercial contacts with Western Asia increased, and there is evidence of trade with Crete and Cyprus.

Impressive pyramids were built for the kings of the Twelfth Dynasty at Lisht, Dahshur, and Fayoum, most of them largely of mud-brick with limestone reinforcing walls and outer casing. Some of the finest examples of ancient Egyptian jewelry were discovered in tombs of royal women at Dahshur and at Lahun in the Fayoum.

The god Amun of Thebes first came to

prominence in the Middle Kingdom, and the first of his many sanctuaries at Karnak was built. The royal sculpture of the latter part of the Twelfth Dynasty is particularly distinctive, with the 'world-weary,' realistic portraits of the kings displaying graphically the responsibility of power as an absolute ruler. Literary works, stories, and philosophical treatises also flourished during this period.

The Thirteenth Dynasty had a large number of kings with short reigns, reminiscent of the end of the Old Kingdom, with real power apparently in the hands of the viziers and provincial governors. Control over Nubia was relaxed, and there was an influx of Asiatics into Lower Egypt. At the start of the Second Intermediate Period there is no evidence of conflict between Egyptians and Asiatics, as later accounts of an 'invasion' allege, but it appears that the Asiatics gradually took over administrative positions in the Delta, increasing their influence until they were able to seize the throne, and form the Fifteenth Dynasty.

Known as the 'Hyksos,' the Greek form of the ancient Egyptian *heka khaswt*, 'rulers of foreign lands,' they ruled from Avaris in the Eastern Delta, although their authority was confined to Lower and Middle Egypt, while the Theban area was ruled by local princes. After 1560 BC, the Seventeenth Dynasty in Thebes managed to extend its control over the whole of southern Egypt and Lower Nubia, and the campaign to expel the Hyksos began. By 1530 BC this had been achieved by Ahmose, first king of the Eighteenth Dynasty, and Egypt was once again a united kingdom. This was the start of a period of imperial expansion, and the high point of ancient Egyptian achievement.

Model of a royal tomb
Limestone
Dynasty 12
L. 36 cm; W. 11 cm; H. 2.72 cm
Dahshur

Stela of Lady Sent-Ites,
Limestone
H. 65 cm; W. 32.5 cm
Dynasty 12–13
Abydos
SR 9437/CG 20017

Two-sided stela
Limestone
H. 52 cm; W. 23 cm.
Dynasty 13
Abydos
SR 9442/CG 20023

**Rectangular stela
of Sobekhotep**
Limestone
W. 18 cm; H. 21cm.
Dynasty 13
Abydos
SR 9135/CG 20353

Painted stela
Limestone
Middle Kingdom
Al-Bersha

37

Ancestor bust of woman
Limestone
W. 9 cm; H. 17.5 cm; D. 6.15 cm
Middle Kingdom
Karnak

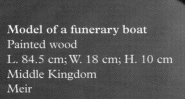

Model of a funerary boat
Painted wood
L. 84.5 cm; W. 18 cm; H. 10 cm
Middle Kingdom
Meir

Jewel box
Ivory
H. 14 cm
Dynasty 18
Tutankhamun Collection

The New Kingdom

(Eighteenth to Twentieth Dynasties)
c. 1550–1086 BC

ith the aim of consolidating their frontiers to the south and northeast, the early kings of the New Kingdom extended Egyptian control over Nubia and much of ancient Syria–Palestine, creating a virtual empire. Peace brought prestige and increased availability of resources through trade, and art and architecture flourished.

The Eighteenth Dynasty is characterized by the acquisition of the empire by the warrior pharaohs, such as Ahmose, Tuthmosis I, and above all Tuthmosis III, and the increasing power and influence of the priesthood of the god Amun-Re of Thebes. Greater political and economic stability allowed for the resumption of trading expeditions to distant lands for luxury goods, and as the general wealth of the country rose, so did schemes for maintaining and exploiting that prosperity.

Kings built temples to their favorite gods, particularly Amun-Re of Thebes, Ptah of Memphis and Re-Harakhte of Heliopolis. In Thebes, the great temple complex of Karnak chronicles the reigns of the kings of the New Kingdom, their military prowess, and their gratitude to the god Amun-Re, who had bestowed their victories and guaranteed their eminence. In Western Thebes a new cemetery was chosen for royal burials, the bleak and remote Valley of the Kings, where it was hoped the kings' tombs and their precious contents would be preserved for eternity. Fate and grave robbers decreed otherwise, but miraculously the tomb of the historically insignificant boy-king Tutankhamun was discovered almost intact in 1922, testifying to the lost magnificence of the burials of greater kings.

The apex of cultural achievement attained

in the reign of Amenhotep III toward the end of the Eighteenth Dynasty was almost eclipsed by his son and successor, Akhenaten, an enigmatic figure, who abandoned the traditional pantheon of Egyptian gods for a form of monotheism centered on the cult of the Aten, the sun disk. The old form of the religion was restored during the reign of his son, Tutankhamun.

In the early Nineteenth Dynasty, Seti I and his son Ramesses II re-established Egyptian prestige in Western Asia, the latter eventually concluding a peace treaty with the Hittites of eastern Anatolia, who had been threatening the northern border of the empire. During his sixty-seven year reign, Ramesses II exemplified the resurgent greatness of Egypt, building a new city in the eastern Delta and many temples throughout the country.

Libyans as well as Western Asiatics continued to threaten Egyptian security, and a new danger, the 'Sea Peoples' from southern Turkey and various east Mediterranean islands, began to advance on Egypt. Moving southward through Syria–Palestine, they were eventually turned back from the borders of Egypt in about 1177 BC by the last of the great warrior pharaohs, Ramesses III of the Twentieth Dynasty.

Under constant pressure from security threats from within and without, the stability of the state rapidly declined under the last of the Ramesside kings at the end of the Twentieth Dynasty. Nubia was detached from Egyptian control, and Herihor took over rule of Upper Egypt as High Priest of Amun, while in Lower Egypt Smendes ruled from Tanis for an ineffectual Ramesses XI. With the collapse of the empire, Egypt was no longer regarded by neighboring countries as the supreme power in the region.

Lid of an alabaster jar
Diameter 13 cm
Dynasty 18
Tutankhamun
    Collection

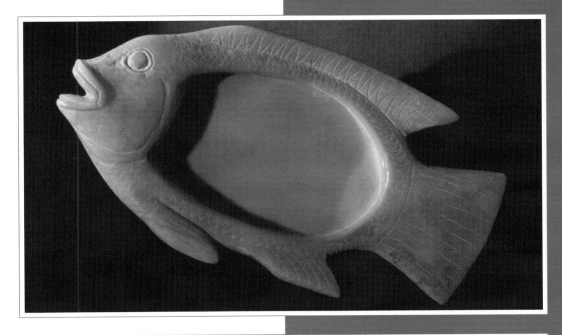

△△ **Spoon in the form of a fish**
Ivory
L. 12 cm; W. 6.1 cm
Dynasty 18, reign of Amenhotep III
French excavation, tomb of Aperia, Saqqara

Small papyrus box
Papyrus fiber
L. 23cm ; W. 23 cm
Dynasty 18
Tutankhamun Collection

Four model boats
Wood
L. papyrus model: 124 cm;
   model with paddle and
   mast: 114 cm; model with
   double-storied cabin 109
   cm; model with smaller
   cabin: 70 cm
Dynasty 18
Tutankhamun Collection

Necklace with falcon pendant
Gold, carnelian, chalcedony,
   colored glass paste
L. 65cm; W. 9cm
Dynasty 18
Tutankhamun Collection

Head of a woman
Wood
W.16 cm; .H. 24 cm
Dynasty 18, reign of Amenhotep III
French excavation, tomb of Aperia, Saqqara

Two measuring rods (ancient Egyptian cubit)
Schist, wood
Schist: L. 52.3 cm; W. 3 cm; H. 1.6 cm
Wood: L. 52.5 cm; W. 2.6 cm; H. 2 cm
Dynasty 18 (1550–1307 BC)
French excavation, tomb of Aperia, Saqqara
Excavation nos. 130, 225, season 1988

Statue of Nakhet
Black granite
H. 44 cm
Dynasty 18, reign of Amenhotep II
Egyptian Museum 14/10/69/4

▷▷ **Naophorous statue of Sebty**
Quartzite
H. 32 cm
Dynasty 18, reign of Amenhotep III
Karnak

Upper part of a statue of a vizier
Quartzite
H. 57 cm
Dynasty 18
Taba

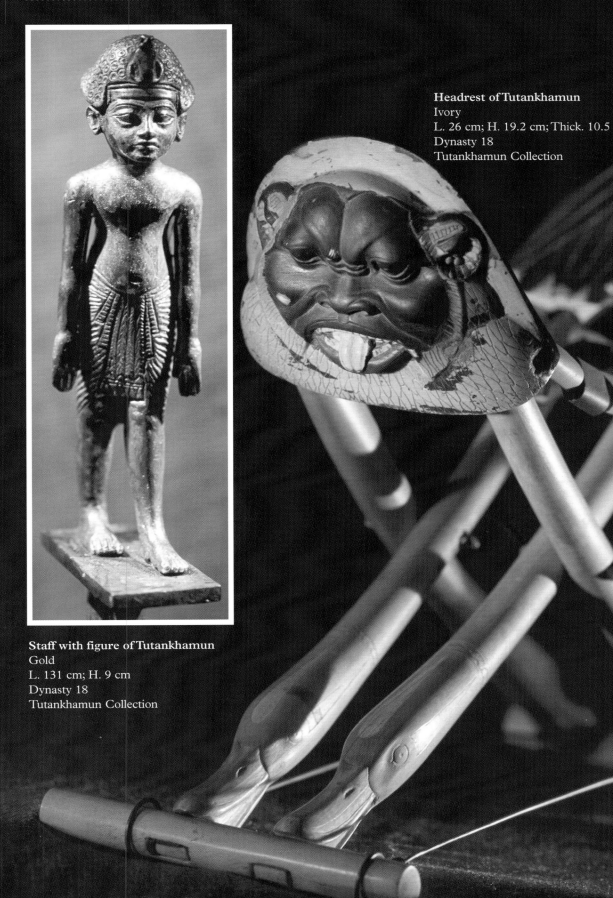

Headrest of Tutankhamun
Ivory
L. 26 cm; H. 19.2 cm; Thick. 10.5
Dynasty 18
Tutankhamun Collection

Staff with figure of Tutankhamun
Gold
L. 131 cm; H. 9 cm
Dynasty 18
Tutankhamun Collection

**Double seated statue of
a man and his wife**
Limestone
H. 75 cm
Dynasty 18
Taba

△△**Pectoral of Tutankhamun**
Gold and semi-precious stones
H. 8.4 cm; W. 6.3 cm
Dynasty 18
Tutankhamun Collection

Fragment of a coffin
Basalt
W. 20 cm; H. 30 cm
Late Dynasty 18
Saqqara
Egyptian Museum

Block showing a woman's face
Limestone
W. 17.5 cm; H. 25.5 cm; D. 3.8 cm
Dynasty 18–19
Found by M. Ibrahim Aly in 1986, Saqqara
Excavation no. 18599aa

Pyramidion of Khonsu-Hori
Painted limestone
H. 45 cm
Dynasty 18–19
Probably from the Theban necropolis
Egyptian Museum

Sphinx of Ramesses II
Limestone
L. 37 cm; W. 9 cm;
H. 18 cm.
Dynasty 19, reign of
Ramesses II
(1304–1237 BC)
Karnak
Egyptian Museum
CG 42146

**Statue of Neb-re as standard-bearer of the goddess
Sekhmet**
Sandstone
H. 123.5 cm
Dynasty 19, reign of Ramesses II
Storehouse no. 26, Zawyet Umm al-Raham, Marsa Matruh

▷ **Naos of the god Ptah and the goddess Sekhmet**
Sandstone
H. 90 cm
Dynasty 19, reign of Ramesses II
Storehouse no. 27, Zawyet Umm al-Raham, Marsa
Matruh

Mummy mask of Sennedjem
Painted cartonnage
Dynasty 19 (1318–1304 BC)
Tomb of Sennedjem, found in 1868
Egyptian Museum

Upper part of a small statue of Seti I
Gray granite
H. 21 cm
Dynasty 19, reign of Seti I (1318–1304 BC)
Temple of Osiris, Abydos
Egyptian Museum CG 751

Statue of Anubis
Limestone
L. 67 cm; W. 25 cm; H. 54 cm
Dynasty 19
Found by P. Munro in 1985, Saqqara
Excavation no. D 3/4–20.86

Statue of Amoneminet
Painted limestone
H. 26 cm
Ramesside Period (1305–1196 BC)
Deir al-Medina
Egyptian Museum JE 43576

Double statue of Amenemipet and his wife
Limestone
Dynasty 19
L. 41 cm; W. 45 cm; H. 84 cm
Found by P. Munro in 1986, Saqqara

▷**Unfinished relief of a king**
Limestone
L. 32 cm; W. 74 cm
New Kingdom

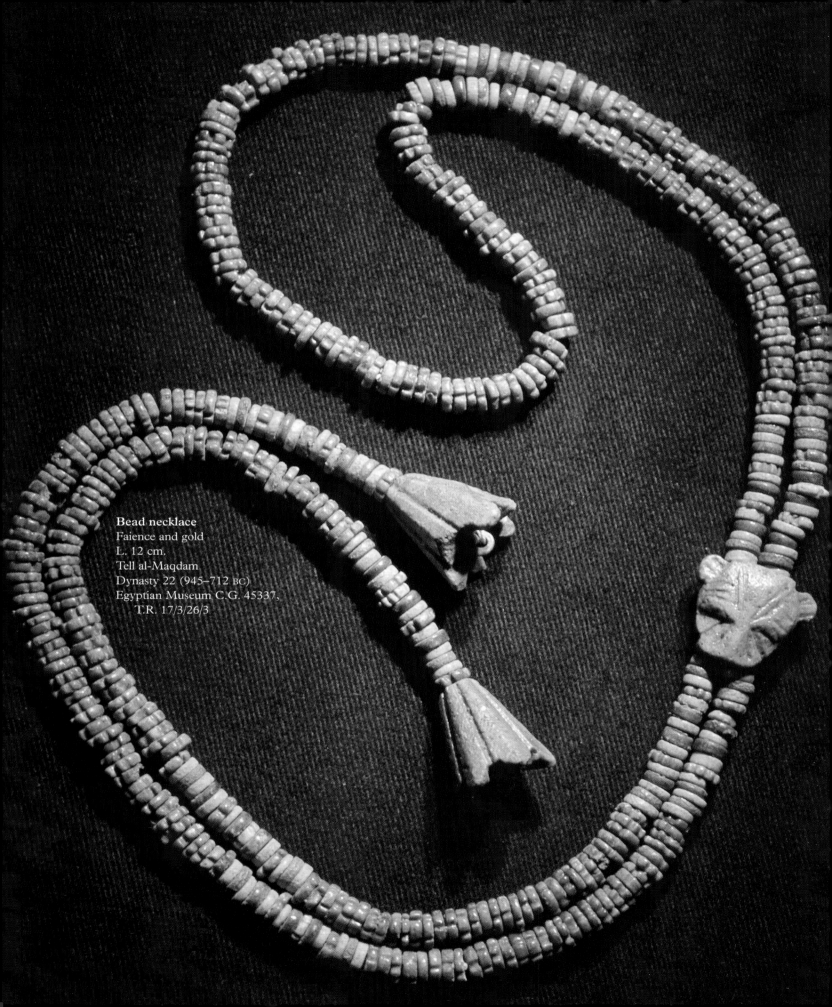

Bead necklace
Faience and gold
L. 12 cm.
Tell al-Maqdam
Dynasty 22 (945–712 BC)
Egyptian Museum C.G. 45337,
 T.R. 17/3/26/3

The Third Intermediate Period, Late Period, and Greco-Roman Period

(Twenty-first to Thirtieth Dynasties, Ptolemaic and Roman Periods) c. 1086 BC – AD 1550

During the Third Intermediate Period the government of the country was divided between kings in Lower Egypt and the High Priests of Amun in Thebes. Power was gradually taken over in the north by officials of Libyan origin, who formed the Twenty-second Dynasty. Egypt split into small kingdoms and principalities, while the Nubian state began to extend its authority over the Nile Valley, eventually taking over the whole country and forming the Twenty-fifth Dynasty. A Nubian princess was appointed as 'divine votaress of Amun' to oversee the loyalty of the Thebans. However, the Nubian pharaohs were unable to withstand the rising power of the Assyrians, who invaded Egypt twice between 667 and 663 BC, sacked Thebes, and drove the Nubians back to their homeland.

The ruling house of the Twenty-sixth Dynasty was backed by the Assyrians and ruled from Sais in the Western Delta. Many Greeks settled in Egypt during this period, either as mercenaries, or for commerce, which was centered on the Greek-style Delta city of Naucratis. Any threat from Nubia was reduced by an Egyptian show of strength, but the northwestern frontier remained vulnerable to attack. The Saite Period saw great appreciation of the classical art styles of the Old Kingdom.

In 525 BC Egypt suffered the first Persian invasion, but after the Persian defeat by the Greeks at Marathon in 490 BC, Persian control in Egypt waned, and the Twenty-eighth Dynasty witnessed a resumption of Egyptian independence for the next sixty years of the Twenty-ninth and Thirtieth Dynasties. The second Persian invasion occurred in 343 BC, and was terminated after ten years by Alexander the

Block statue, probably a priest of Osiris
Limestone
H. 33 cm
Dynasty 22–23 (945–712 BC)
Tanta Museum 3368

Great, who was welcomed by the Egyptians as a deliverer from Persian oppression.

For the next three hundred years Egypt was ruled by Macedonian Greeks. After the death of Alexander in 323 BC, his general Ptolemy became the founder of the Ptolemaic dynasty, which ended with the suicide of the famous Cleopatra VII in 30 BC. Under the Ptolemies there was a renewal of Egyptian influence, especially with regard to the newly-founded port city of Alexandria. Ptolemy I and II created the monuments for which the city was famous, including the Pharos lighthouse, and the great scholastic academy, the Museon and Library. Greek gods were worshiped alongside their Egyptian counterparts, or were assimilated with them, there was a synthesis of Greek and Egyptian culture, and Greek became the language of the administration. On the death of Cleopatra, Egypt became a province of the Roman Empire, but with exceptional status as the personal property of the emperor himself.

Like the Ptolemies, the Roman emperors were regarded by the Egyptians as the successors to the pharaohs, and were depicted as such in carvings and sculptures. Some of the finest examples of ancient temples survive almost intact from the Greco-Roman period. Egypt remained a province of the Roman empire until AD 395, when it came under Byzantine rule.

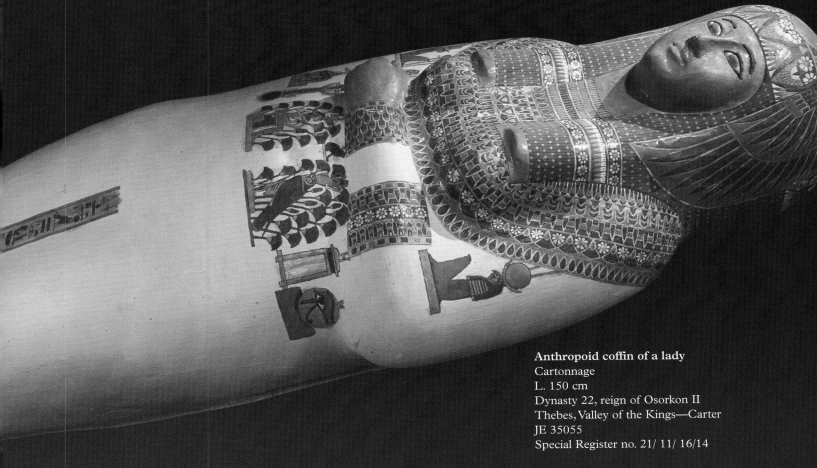

Anthropoid coffin of a lady
Cartonnage
L. 150 cm
Dynasty 22, reign of Osorkon II
Thebes, Valley of the Kings—Carter
JE 35055
Special Register no. 21/ 11/ 16/14

Statue of Ptah-Sokar-Osiris
Colored wood
H. 62cm
End of Third Intermediate Period
Tomb 99, West Bank, Luxor

Serapeum stela of Pa Ka
Limestone
H.16.1 cm; W. 9.3 cm; D. 2,4 cm.
Dynasty 26 (664–525 BC)
Memphite Serapeum
Excavation no. 18474

Gold artifacts
Dynasty 26
Tomb of Naasa,
    wife of Djed Khonsu
Bahariya Oasis

Amulet of Kebeh-senu-ef
Gold
H. 9cm
Dynasty 26
Bahariya Oasis

**Fragment of hieroglyphic stela
    of Ahmose-mery-netjer**
Limestone
H. 19.9 cm; W. 15.5 cm; D. 3.1 cm
Dynasty 26–27
Great Vaults, Memphite Serapeum.
Excavation no. 18389

Statue of Padiamunnebneuttawy
L. 60cm; W. 36 cm
End of Dynasty 30
Egyptian Museum CG 48611

Sphinx of Psammetichus 1
H. 47 cm
Saite period, reign of Psammetichus I or II,
    around 664 BC
Egyptian Museum CG. 48603

Stela to the god Osiris
Sandstone
L. 60cm; W. 38 cm
Dynasty 30 (380–343 BC)
Egyptian Museum

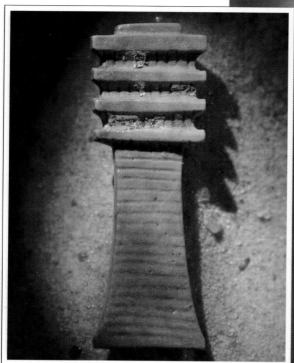

Djed pillar
Gilded faience
H. 7.5 cm
Late Period
Cat. no 1113, Tell Basta

Statue of the god Bes
Limestone
W. 60 cm; H.137 cm
Late Period
Bahariya Oasis

Two shrew sarcophagi
Gilded limestone
L. 17 cm; W. 10.5 cm; H. 8.5 cm;
    L. of interior 11.5 cm;
    W. of interior 3 cm.
L. 11 cm; W. 6 cm; H. 5.8 cm;
    L. of interior 9 cm;
    W. of interior 4.5 cm.
Abydos
Late Period
Excavation nos. 940, 942

Statue of Bast
Bronze
Bubastis
Late Period (6th–4th cent. BC)
Egyptian Museum

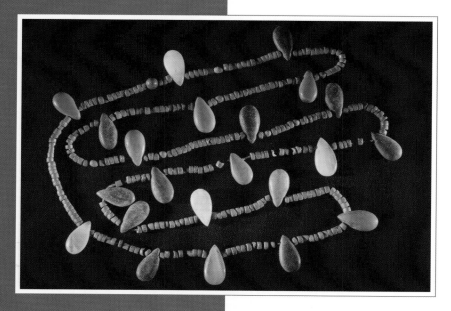

**Statue of the Apis bull and the lower part of a man
    holding a vessel**
Black granite
H. 69 cm
Late Period
Karnak Cachette

△**Necklace**
Glass, faience, and semi-precious beads
Late Period
Egyptian Museum TR 5/27/8/6

Mummy of a 5-year-old boy
L. 84 cm; W. 27 cm
Late Period
Bahariya Oasis

Mummy of a 4-year-old girl
L. 84 cm; W. 28 cm
Late Period
Bahariya Oasis

**Anthropoid coffin of the Lady
    Taberu**
Cartonnage
L. 160 cm; W. 42 cm; H. 28 cm
Late Period

Statue of the goddess Isis suckling the infant Horus
Late Period (6th–4th cent. BC)
Egyptian Museum

Six painted pottery vessels
270 BC
Meir

⩞ **Sphinx**
L. 103 cm; W. 35 cm; H. 60 cm
Dynasty 30 or early Ptolemaic Period
Egyptian Museum

Stela from Akhmim
Black granite
L. 55.6 cm; W. 31 cm
350–300 BC
Akhmim
Egyptian Museum 34095

Mummy mask
Gilded cartonnage
H. 42.5 cm
Ptolemaic Period
Saqqara, Cat. no. 98

A mummy mask
Cloth and painted plaster
L. 44 cm; W. 23 cm
Greco-Roman Period
Middle Egypt
Egyptian Museum

Statue of Isis
Granite
H. head: 45 cm; chest: 59 cm;
    trunk: 79 cm;
     base and foot: 40 cm.
Late Ptolemaic Period
Abu Qir, 2001

Funerary stela
Limestone
W 30 cm; H. 20 cm
Roman Period (2nd–3rd cent. AD)
Kom Abu Billo (Terenuthis)
Discovered in 1935

Stela of the Emperor Tiberius
Sandstone
Roman period
W. 35cm; H. 51cm
Egyptian museum CG. 9268